We're off on an amazing...

Alphabet

abcdef
ghijklmnop
qrstuvwxyz

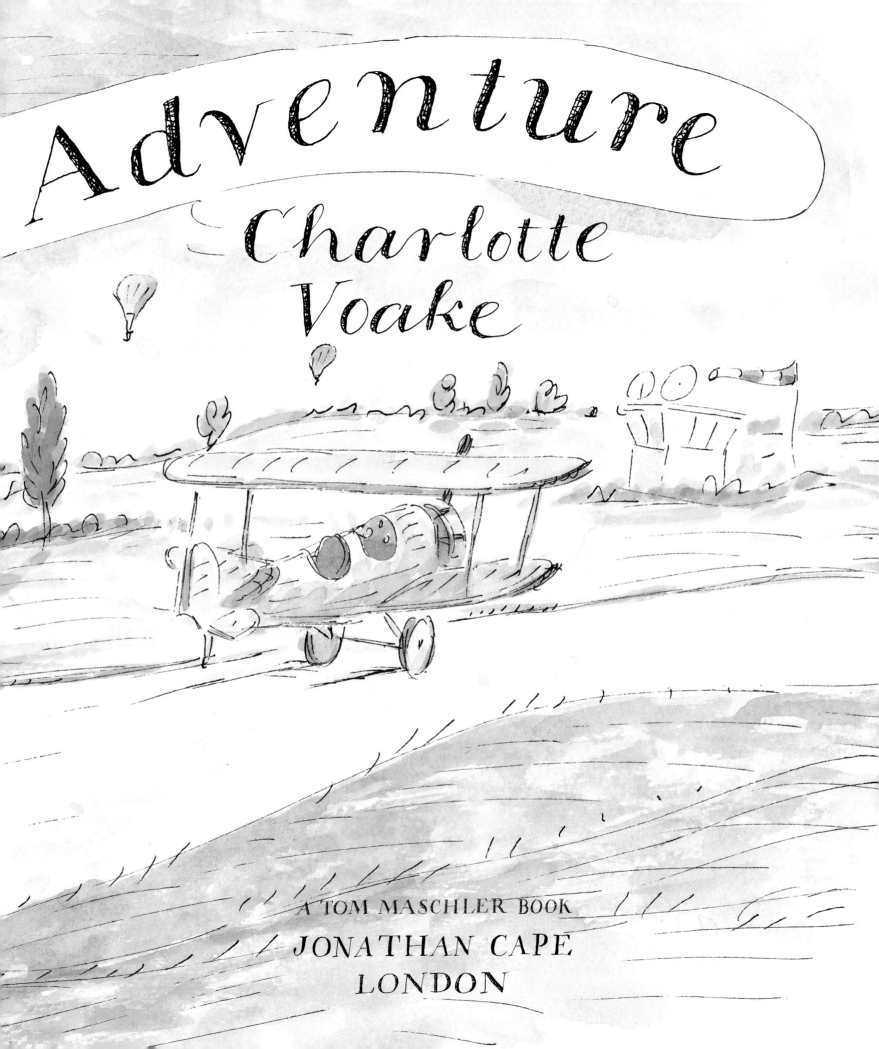

Adventure

Charlotte Voake

A TOM MASCHLER BOOK

JONATHAN CAPE

LONDON

Come with us and we will see...

an Atlas and an anchor,

a Boy in a brown basket a blue balloon, and a pair of binoculars

a Crumbling Castle and a cake with candles

a Dog looking down at some ducks

(extraordinary) Eggs belonging to an enormous eagle

Ferns in the forest

Girls in the green grass and a goose

a Hat

and some hens

Some Interesting Instruments

and a Juggler in the jungle

a Key lost on a Lilypad in a Large lake

Masses of moths

Nestlings in their nest.

Orange oranges in a boat

Plenty of penguins plunging

a Quarrel at the quarry

Rain on a red roof

Stormy skies and
a statue in the sea

Tall towers and
terrible traffic

Uncle Umberto looking at
the View of the village

Wet washing in
windy weather

X-ray and a
xylophone

Yellow Yachts

and ZEBRAS

And look out for....

1 ONE OCTOPUS
2 TWO TABLES
3 THREE TREES
4 FOUR FLOWERS
5 FIVE FLIES

6 SIX STARS
7 SEVEN SEAGULLS
8 EIGHT EGGS
9 NINE NESTLINGS
10 TEN TUGBOATS

Aa Bb Cc Dd Ee F

Jj Kk Ll Mn
Ss Tt

Gg Hh Ii Rr
Nn Oo Pp Qq
Uu Vv Ww Xx Yy Zz

Aa

anchor

alphabet

aeroplane

Bb

burner

beard

balloon

bird

C c

clouds

castle

cannons

cat

doors

dragon

Dd

drawbridge

DOWN TO THE DUNGEONS

DANGER

E e   evening

eagle

eggs

F f

forest

flies

flowers

Gg

giraffe

grass

girls

Hh

hills

handstand   houses

hens

I i

islands

insects

instruments

ice cream

jet

jungle

J j

jug

jelly

Kk

kites

kimono

kittens

kiss

key

Mm

moon

mountain

map

moths

N n

night

nuts

nest

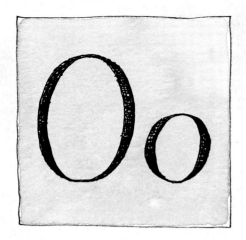

Oo

ocean

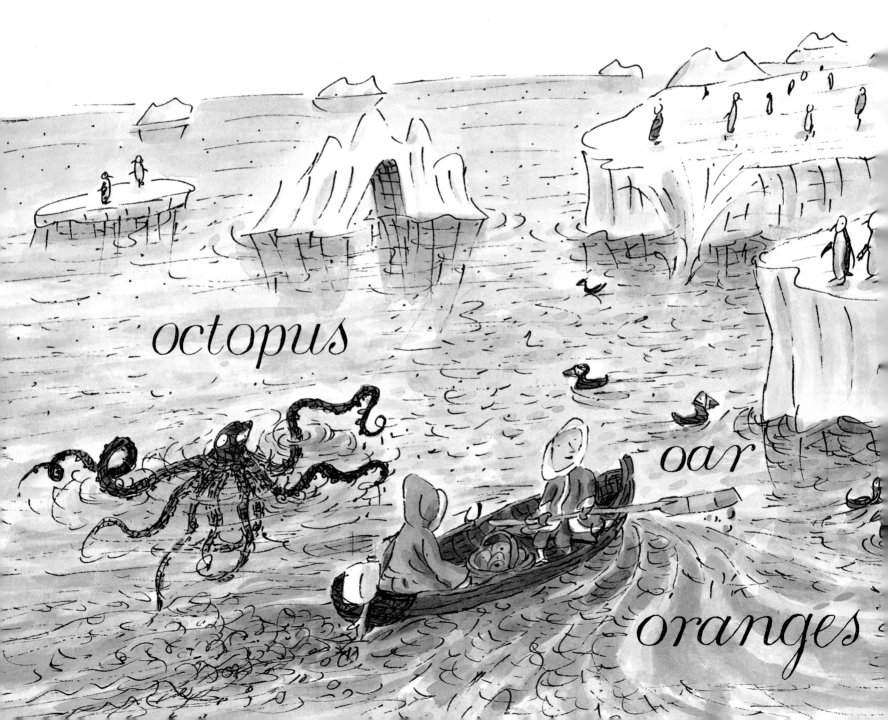

octopus

oar

oranges

P p

pole

penguins

puffin

rainbow

road

rabbits

Rr

S s

skyscraper

statue

street

T t

tanker

tower

trees

Uu

umbrella

uniform

unicycle

uncle

V v

volcano

valley   village

viaduct

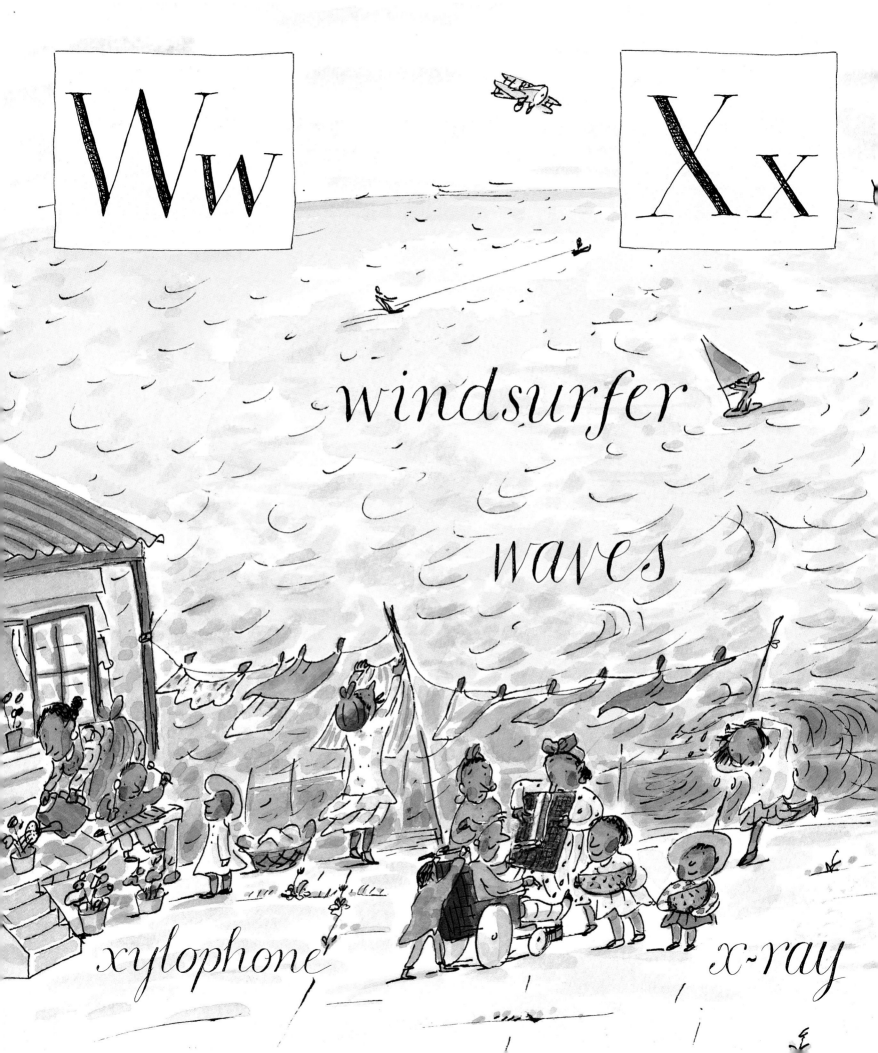

W w

X x

windsurfer

waves

xylophone

x-ray

yachts

Y y

yams

yawn

yo-yo